Where Hands Belong

Written by:
Mira Collins

Illustrated by:
Ram D. Santos

Dear Parents

Author Note

Dear Reader,

I've chosen to write this book under a pen name — not because I'm hiding, but because I'm healing.

Like many children, I once felt silenced, confused, and scared, As a survivor of childhood sexual abuse, protecting my privacy is one of the ways I've reclaimed my voice.

But this book isn't about me — it's about your child, It's about giving families the tools to start honest, loving conversations that can protect and empower. My hope is that these pages help kids feel safe, seen, and strong — the way every child deserves to feel.

If even one child finds the courage to speak up, or one parent learns how to listen differently — then this book has done its job. Thank you for being here. Thank you for caring.

With all my heart, Mira Collins (pen name)

For my favorite little human –
Your courage fills me with pride. You are, and always will be, the reason I found my voice.

Now that I'm growing, I've learned when to say "No."
But there's still more I'm learning each day—
Like which kinds of touch are okay to stay.

My parents taught me ten rules to know,
And I want to share them wherever I go.
I keep them with me, both day and night—
They help me feel safe. They help me choose right.

I remember rule number one when I'm in doubt.
Here's what it's always all about:
#1) You're the boss of your body—no one else.
You get to choose for your very self.
If someone touches and you feel upset,
You can say "no" without regret.
Stand up strong, let your feelings show,
Then lift your head—and off you go.

Rule number two is to remind you and me,
That private parts are not for others to see.
#2) Our bodies deserve our love and care—
They're special and private, not something to share.

EXIT

Rule number three might not bring cheer,
But it's a rule we all should hear.
#3) Games aren't for touching or kissing too—
If it feels wrong, it's a big clue.
Private means private, right from the start.
If something feels off, trust your heart.

Shh, it's time to share what's true.
Here comes rule number four for you:
#4) If a secret makes you feel sad or scared,
Tell someone safe who's kind and prepared.
Never keep quiet when something feels wrong
Your voice is brave, your heart is strong.

We must be kind and care for each other,
Like a family — like sisters and brothers.
#5) Touching someone else's
body parts is not okay.
and you have
the right to run away.

If a touch feels wrong or makes you feel mixed,
Trust your gut and use rule number six.

#6) Say no to touch that doesn't feel right,
Even when someone puts up a fight.
Your body is precious—so is your choice.
You don't owe a hug, a kiss, or a voice.

Use rule number seven when
you need your space.

Being alone is not out of place.
#7) No one should watch while you
change or bathe.

That's your time, your place, your safe
escape.
Privacy matters, it's not just polite
It's your right to keep those moments out of
sight.

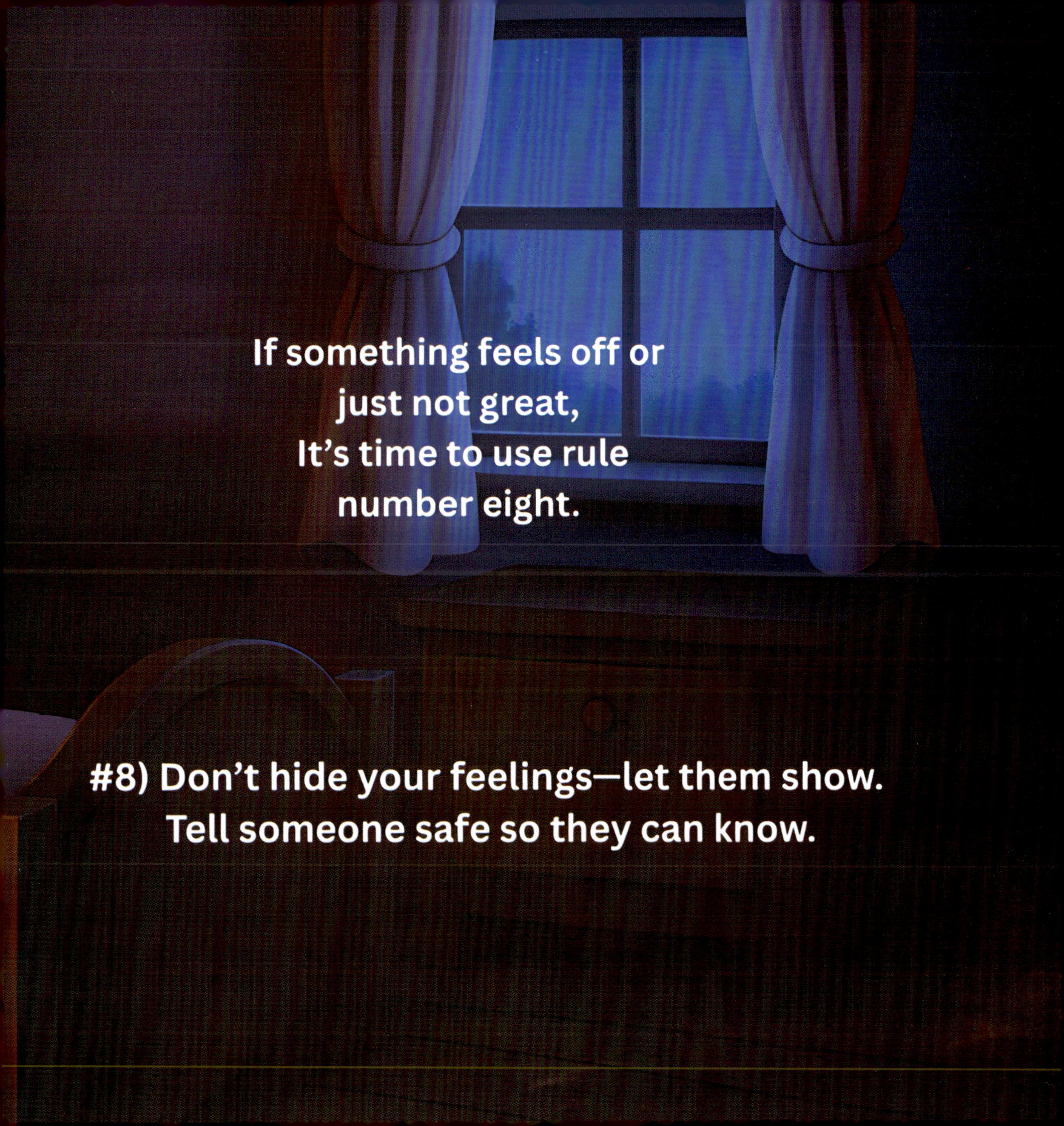

If something feels off or
just not great,
It's time to use rule
number eight.

**#8) Don't hide your feelings—let them show.
Tell someone safe so they can know.**

Rule number nine helps you stay strong.
When something feels off or just feels wrong.

#9) Find someone safe who knows what to do.
They'll help you feel better and stand by you.

Here we are now at rule number ten.
Remember these rules again and again.

#10) Hands are for helping, not for harm—
If something feels wrong, raise the alarm.

Resources For Adults

As a caregiver, ensuring your child's safety is always a top priority— and one of the most powerful ways to do that is by teaching them about body safety and consent.
These topics are essential for helping kids understand their rights, recognize unsafe situations, and make confident, informed decisions about their bodies. When taught early and discussed regularly, body safety education becomes a vital tool in preventing abuse.

Statistics from the National Child Traumatic Stress Network (2020) show that approximately 1 in 4 girls and 1 in 6 boys experience sexual abuse before turning 18, By helping children identify safe vs. unsafe touch, set personal boundaries, and conlidentiy say "no," we give them tools to speak up and seek help when needed.

It's also crucial for adults to stay informed – learning to spot warning signs, understand prevention strategies, and take action when something isn't right, With greater awareness, we can better protect the children in our care and help create a safer world for them.

Ask the Hard Questions

One of the most effective ways to teach body safety is by having honest, ongoing conversations with our children. These talks not only help us understand what they already know, but also give us space to introduce new ideas or reinforce key lessons.

Using open-ended questions encourages children to think critically and express themselves more freely. It's important to approach these conversations without blame or fear - our goal is to empower them, build trust, and help them feel eonfident recognizing and responding to uncomfortable situations.

Below are sample questions you can use as a guide. Feel free to personalize them based on your child's age and understanding:

- "How does it feel to say'No' when something doesn't feel right?"
- "Why do you think learning to say 'No' helps keep you safe?"
- "What would you do if someone touched you in a way that made you feel upset or unsure?"
- "If someone asked you to keep a secret that made you feel weird or scared, what would you do?"
- "What should you do if someone tries to touch a part of your body that's private?"
- "Can you think of ways to keep your body safe at home, school, or anywhere you go?"
- "Why is it important to talk to a grown-up you trust if something doesn't feel okay?"
- "What are some body safety rules that everyone should know and follow?"

Spot unsafe behavior early

As parents and caregivers, it's essential to recognize how individuals who abuse children often operate – not just to respond to danger, but to prevent it. Many perpetrators of child sexual abuse don't rely on physical force. Instead, they use manipulation, emotional influence, or subtle forms of coercion to gain a child's trust and keep them silent.

This process is known as grooming – a calculated effort to build a connection with a child in order to exploit them, Grooming may involve giving gifts, sharing secrets, making promises, or offering special attention – all to lower a child's guard and create confusion about boundaries.

Research from the National Child Traumatic Stress Network (2015) shows that most abusers are not strangers, In fact, many are family members, peers, or trusted individuals who have regular access to the child through places like the home, school, religious settings, or social circles.

Rather than using threats or violence, these individuals often rely on their relationship with the child or their position of authority to make the behavior seem “normal” or acceptable. This is part of why abuse can go unnoticed for so long – it's masked by familiarity and trust.

According to a 2012 study by David Finkelhor, around 40% of children who experience sexual abuse are harmed by someone they know – including other children, This shows why it's so important for adults to understand that abuse isn't always committed by a “predator” stereotype, It can happen in close, familiar spaces – and being aware of the signs is key to protecting our kids.

References

- Briere, J., & Elliott, D, M, (2003). Prevalence and psychological sequelae of self-reported childhood physical and sexual abuse. Child Abuse & Neglect, 27(10), 1205-1222. https://doi,org/10.1016/j.chiabu.2003.09.008

- Finkelhor, D. (2009). The prevention of childhood sexual abuse. The Future of children, 19(2), 169-194, https://doi.org/10.1353/foc.0.0035

- Walsh, K, Zwi, K,, Woolfenden, S., & shionsky, A. (2015). School-based education programmes for the prevention of child sexual abuse. Cochrane Database of Systematic Reviews, (4), CD004380. https://doi.org/10.1002/14651858.CD004380.pub3

- Wurtele, s. K., & Kenny, M, c. (2010). Partnering with parents to prevent childhood sexual abuse. Child Abuse Review, 19(2), 130-152. https://doi.org/10.1002/car.1112